WHAT IS A CHRISTIAN?

The Simple, Powerful, and Effective Method of
Three Square Evangelism

John Krivak

Charleston, AR:
COBB PUBLISHING
2020

What is a Christian? The Simple, Powerful, and Effective Method of Three Square Evangelism is copyright ©2020, John Krivak. All rights reserved. No portion of this book may be reproduced in any way (whether digital, audio, photocopy, electronic, or any other method) without the written permission of the author.

Volume discounts are available through the publisher.

All Scripture references are from the New American Standard Bible (NASB). Used with permission.

Published in the United States of America by:
Cobb Publishing
704 E. Main St.
Charleston, AR 72933
www.CobbPublishing.com
CobbPublishing@gmail.com
479.747.8372

ISBN: 978-1-947622-47-0

FOREWORD

Sometimes you ask yourself, "What took me so long?"

That's the feeling I got as I read through John Krivak's manuscript. For so long, I felt like I had to be able to convert people by showing the fallacy of the "sinner's prayer" (it isn't biblical) and proving that baptism was immersion in water that resulted in salvation (which it is).

But my picture, my approach, was incomplete.

The method of evangelism that John presents in this book is not just another method among methods. Instead, it completely changes the focus of evangelism from the skills and knowledge of the teacher to the love and sacrifice of the Savior—and points them to the logical response.

Reading through this book left me convicted of my shortfalls in my attempts to share the gospel with others one-on-one.

But more importantly, it gave me clarity and hope and relief. Yes, relief. Because it showed me how easy it is to point people to Jesus and let *Him* do the converting.

The method in this book is completely biblical.

The method in this book results in stronger converts with deeper commitment to the Lord.

The method in this book is simple, powerful, and Jesus-focused.

And I sit here wishing that John had written this book twenty years ago.

Bradley S. Cobb
February, 2020

For Mark Silas Howell,

Presider over my wedding to Becky,

Presider over our baptisms into Christ Jesus,

Evangelist who set our course by sermon, class, example and fellowship.

Galatians 6:6 into eternity!

GOOD AND SHORT

I want to offer you a book that gives an effective method of evangelism, and I want it to be good and short.

A *short* book, because you get the basic necessities for successful evangelism, quick and easy. The method is simple. It requires no materials or technology—other than a Bible. It can be worked anytime and anywhere and with anyone. The demands on you are kept small and manageable. You don't need to be an expert in Bible. You won't be asked to recall much from memory. This method is easily mastered because it follows a logical flow. The pieces fit nicely and make sense. After all, evangelism is not rocket science!

A *good* book, because it achieves quality results. Evangelism must be done well. Jesus was critical of bad workmanship when converting other people: *"...you travel around on sea and land to make one [convert]; and when he becomes one, you make him twice as much a son of hell as yourselves!"* (Matthew 23:15).

That rebuke aimed at Judaism. However, Christians who evangelize shoddily also produce failure, as seen in their converts. Effective evangelistic work—bringing outsiders into Christian fellowship—needs to produce converts of the quality God requires. Quality counts, and this method achieves that.

I can teach you.

You will come away with a clear understanding of what it takes to do the job competently, and you will know how to do it. And the demands made of you will be minimal. You will be shown how to unleash the power God provides.

<u>This method is not a gimmick</u>. It works because we are careful to accomplish all that a true conversion truly demands.

I'll present the method in an easy three-part system: Squares One, Two, and Three. It is easy and uncomplicated. But take note of this: around the basic core, early in the book, I'll add "extra" discussion of the inner workings—strategy, psychological impact, spiritual dynamics, and much more. Don't be overwhelmed by this. When it comes time to work the method in an actual evangelistic encounter, all you need is the core. The "extra" will merely provide helpful background information. Later in the book, we will strip away the extra discussion to focus on the pure simplicity of the method—and it is quite simple.

You can do this!

SQUARE ONE

Where We Find FOCUS

"Let your eyes look directly ahead and let your gaze be fixed straight in front of you."

—Proverbs 4:25 (NASB)

"Focus is a matter of deciding what things you're not going to do."

—John Carmack

You are at Square One when you have a person ready to hear the gospel. He or she may be happy to listen, and may have even invited your presentation. Or, your friend may be curious enough to listen after you extended the invitation. You arrive at Square One when you have someone ready to listen. Later, we will offer a few insights on getting to Square One.

We begin by setting a question before the convert: *"What is a Christian?"*

Oh, the power in that little question! It looks so simple and so easy to answer correctly. Like a laser-beam, its power resides in its ability to focus the scope of the discussion. So many evangelistic encounters fail because they lose focus, wandering off into distractions and less important issues. Evangelism is about making Christians—shouldn't we begin with a shared understanding of what a Christian is? The question points us in the right direction.

The question is deceptively simple, and we will accept only one answer as correct. Everyone thinks they know what a Christian is! The only acceptable answer is this:

"A Christian is a person who has a saving relationship with God through Jesus Christ."

No other answer will do!

Requiring this specific answer focuses direction forward in two ways.

First, it settles the "religion vs. relationship" approaches to conversion in a decidedly relational direction. We are working to establish a covenant-relationship—specifically, the New Covenant—between the convert and God.

A second benefit is introduced when the convert, as is quite typical, simply cannot answer the question correctly! He or she wonders: *"Perhaps I never really understood what a Christian actually is?"*

This introduces doubt that is quite helpful toward creating an open-minded disposition—and especially so if the convert already claims to be a Christian.

In driving for the correct answer, we are going to play **DOING** against **BEING.** *Distinguishing between DOING and BEING is essential to this method!* A few hypothetical encounters between you (Y) and the convert (C) will demonstrate how to work this procedure:

Y. What is a Christian?

C. Well, a Christian is someone who believes in Jesus and the Bible.

Y. Believing Jesus and the Bible is something a Christian DOES, but that doesn't tell us what a Christian IS. Can you try again?

Y. What is a Christian?

C. Well, a Christian is someone who obeys Jesus and follows His teaching.

Y. Those are very important things that a Christian DOES. But again, that doesn't tell us what a Christian IS.

Someone familiar with the churches of Christ might answer as follows:

Y. What is a Christian?

C. A Christian is one who hears, believes, repents, confesses, and is baptized!

Y. Those are all things a person must DO to become a Christian, but that does not tell us what a Christian IS! Try again?

Your job has been to create doubt in the convert. That may make you uncomfortable; and it may be even worse for your convert!

Every new attempt to answer brings the same repeated negative evaluation—to a question that seems so easy and simple.

Frustration soon turns to exasperation: *"OK—I give up! YOU tell me what a Christian IS!"*

Let this technique have its effect, no matter how discomforting for both of you. Make the convert work for the only right answer! The frustration, no matter how bad it feels, is doing its work and it will have a positive effect. It pulls the rug from under confidence in a few RELIGIOUS acts, and from under any who think salvation is about a "completed checklist." You have made it quite uncomfortable to believe that way any longer.

You have placed the only acceptability in *"…a saving relationship with God through Jesus Christ."*

If you have driven the convert to sheer exasperation, he or she should be all ears!

A relationship with Jesus is amazing! *When love and faithfulness flow between relational partners—Jesus toward you, then from you toward Jesus—salvation happens. This is covenant.* Two pledge to one another: love without limit and loyalty that never fails—then they watch each other with eagle-eyes for signs of success or failure. It is a living, growing, and dynamic process—and our job is to get our converts to engage Jesus in relationship. *Salvation is found nowhere else—not in religion, not in moral living, not in careful personal development.* This method has one clear focus.

The more you work The Question, the easier and more natural it becomes. Practice as often as possible. Ask family, friends, and co-workers if you can practice on them (you may get a conversion out of it). Keep a lively sense of humor inside yourself as the technique plays out. Each unique person can bring surprise and unpredictability. You will be challenged by creative attempts to find the right answer, then to evaluate each one fairly, and at last to respond in a way that moves the process forward.

Enjoy the challenge! Trust God, and trust the process. Learn from each encounter. You will be more comfortable and skilled after your first ten attempts. It is normal to feel anxious and uncomfortable at first. You will soon see good results, and you will begin to eagerly anticipate the next exciting opportunity.

Do not fail to see the powerful accomplishment that takes place at Square One! By careful technique, the process now has a single focus: relationship with God through Jesus! If our Question and Answer strategy works to achieve this, then it is worth whatever frustration and exasperation it probably caused. You are exactly where you need to be to move to a successful conversion.

Pretty easy so far? Just a little Q&A. You are ready for Square Two!

SQUARE TWO

Where We Find POWER

"For I am not ashamed of the gospel, for it is the power of God for salvation...."

—Romans 1:16 (NASB)

"Power gravitates to the man who knows how."

—Orison Swett Marden

The power in the process is right here.

It is at Square Two that we introduce the Cross, the crucifixion of Jesus. When you do that, you can pretty much step aside and let Jesus take over. Jesus brings the power.

And we need power, don't we? We all feel inadequate. Sometimes I just need a fresh reading of 2 Corinthians. In this comforting Scripture, Paul drops his "apostolic superhero persona" and admits fears, weakness, and inadequacy. He carries the powerful gospel of Jesus, but it's like putting treasure (the gospel) in a jar of clay. Paul sees himself as the clay jar—fragile, weak, easily broken. But evangelistic ministry teaches him not to rely on his own personal power. Paul learns to draw from God's power (1:8; 4:7; 6:7; 12:9; 13:4).

You are going to learn to rely on God's power—to *"let go and let God!"*

Let me share some lessons I learned from past failures. Unfocussed efforts allowed the direction of discussion to go all over the place. That put upon me the burden and pressure of being a "Bible expert" able to answer all questions. But even when I met these challenges, conversion seldom resulted!

You can win arguments without winning hearts.

The method in this book takes pressure off you! How? By pointing the "relational focus" to the crucifixion of Jesus (that is, to the gospel)! *When you set the Cross before your convert, power is released.* The interaction is no longer between the convert and you. You introduce Jesus, and step aside to watch the powerful Savior win the victory.

My early attempts at evangelism were exhausting, like I had to dismantle every obstacle and answer every objection. *When I managed to get a baptism, it felt like I had arm-twisted my convert—what effort and work that required!* Eventually I discovered that God put power for that *in the gospel.* Now all I had to do was to get out of the way and let God take over. So how is this to be accomplished?

Now that we have established salvation to require a "saving relationship," we are going to say:

> *For any relationship to work, it requires effort from both partners—right? Let's begin with God's contribution, OK? What God gives to make this work is the death of His Son. That happened when Jesus was crucified.*

This establishes the need for a two-way relationship. Anything less would fail to be truly Christian! God is building a "covenant" with us. God is not merely trying to turn us into "good people" who recognize a code of morality and carefully live by it. He gets no satisfaction in simply having us become "religious people." God is unimpressed when we carefully tick all boxes off a checklist. Without a relationship, all of this counts for nothing—morality, religion, or achievement! Just ask a Pharisee!

The Meaning of the Cross

Now, the Cross must be explained relationally to show what God brings to make this all work. I like to use a little story,

> *A king ruled during time of famine and starvation. He made it law that grain be rationed at one cup per person per day, and anyone caught taking more was to be whipped with 20 lashes.*

One day, those who took more were set aside for punishment. Among them, an old woman who was discovered to be the king's mother! The king was now in a dilemma. If he had his own mother whipped as law required, he would be viewed as cruel and heartless. However, if he let her go, he would be charged with injustice or favoritism!

To resolve the dilemma, the king took off his own royal robes and took the 20 lashes on his own back! That is what Jesus did when He died on the Cross. He took the punishment we deserved, meeting the demands of love and of justice.

What the king did for his mother, Jesus did for us! The story makes a deep impression. With that still fresh, explain the dilemma that our sin creates for God. Simply explain the essence of Genesis 3 (don't develop a full Bible study; this only takes a few minutes). God is pure in holiness and we too must be holy to enjoy fellowship with God. To keep us pure, God attached the death penalty to sin. But Satan led a rebellion against God, starting with Adam & Eve, and eventually all of us fell into sin, immorality, and wrongdoing. The result is that our relationship with God was broken. We all came under penalty of death!

This put God in a dilemma. His justice demanded that sin—*our sin!*—be punished with death. But God's love could not allow that to happen. So God became a human being, and His name was Jesus. Although Jesus was without sin, He suffered death on the Cross as our substitute—just like the king in the story! The penalty for our sins was paid and we could now be forgiven.

Our Response to the Cross

This was what God gave to bring relational success with us, for He so loved the world! And the Cross begs for a response—and the convert should be pressed to answer: *"If Jesus gave His life to make this work, what should we be required to give in return?"*

Again, there is only one valid answer and most people get that without coaxing: *"We must give our lives in return!"* Something very powerful happens right here. The process of this method was, at the beginning, between you and the convert. No longer!

You are no longer involved; you have stepped aside. Now, the convert stands face-to-face with Jesus! They are transacting a relationship together on the basis of His crucifixion. The demands placed on the convert are the demands of Jesus! In Galatians 3:1, Paul reminded the Christians of their saving encounter, *"before whose eyes Jesus Christ was publicly portrayed as crucified."* Awareness of the Crucifixion brings obligation. You have just set the Cross before the eyes of your convert!

Something else just here: you have just obligated the convert with "a demand of greatest magnitude" (actually, Jesus has done that). Jesus demands unlimited self-sacrifice (because that is what He gives us). To validate this demand, we turn the Bible to Luke 9:23-27 and 57-62. This establishes that Jesus requires total commitment from His covenant partner. He demands total self-sacrifice as the only fair reciprocation for the Cross.

Do not be tempted to lessen this demand; insist that it be met in full—otherwise no relationship is possible with Jesus. I call this demand "THE MAGNITUDE OF THE STEP." No one becomes a Christian by making minor adjustments! Step big, or don't step at all.

You may wonder at the wisdom of this, that maybe there will be few takers to an offer whose cost is so high? Actually, the demand will appeal to people because it declares the extraordinary value of the relationship (just as high relational demands actually appeal to couples about to marry). I once had a friend who offered puppies free to a good home. The ad drew zero responses! He reposted the ad, offering the same puppies for $40 apiece. They were all placed in days! Why? Because people are willing to sacrifice much to get something that is worth much. *Make the convert take the big step.*

The Scripture discussed in this paragraph is not part of our method; this is just for your benefit and understanding. Jesus used twin parables to communicate "the magnitude of the step" in Matthew 13:44-46—the hidden treasure and the pearl of great price. Each presents a huge treasure that is available to anyone, but only on one condition: *willingness to sacrifice EVERYTHING to get the treasure!*

I once was evangelizing and declared openly that the convert's life, if given to Jesus, might involve all kinds of hardship, sacrifice, and suffering. Overhearing all this, my wife declared, *"John, most people sugarcoat the offer of salvation—you dip it in lemon!"* Most evangelistic methods are not this honest. You can be honest about the "downside" of Christianity because the upside of a relationship with God is of such surpassing value. The big step is worth taking!

All of this reveals the power that goes to work at Square Two—it really is a marvel! You see this most obviously when converts actually begin to think seriously about taking the big step—total self-surrender before the Cross of Jesus. What power is this? Romans 1:16-17 tells us:

> *For I am not ashamed of the gospel, for it is the power of God for salvation to everyone who believes, to the Jew first and also to the Greek. For in it the righteousness of God is revealed from faith to faith; as it is written, "BUT THE RIGHTEOUS man SHALL LIVE BY FAITH."*

The power is also revealed *by what you don't see!* When evangelizing with your own power (instead of using God's power), using strength and pressure by any means to get a conversion, you tend to almost provoke "pushback"—resistance, dodging, excuses, and diversionary tactics:

- *Do I really have to abandon my addictions and sinful living?*
- *What about the dinosaurs and evolution?*
- *Do I really have to break off sinful relationships?*
- *Isn't this really just your interpretation of the Bible?*
- *Do I really need to be baptized to be saved?*

Set before the powerful Cross, it all wilts. Now, if such thoughts are even entertained secretly, they are not brought up! I can't guarantee absolutely no pushback will come, but this approach has remarkable power to subdue that.

Now let's resume the method—after two readings from Luke 9, I turn to 14:25-27. This reiterates the "magnitude of the step" in two ways.

First, it insists that Jesus must win any "competition among relationships." He ranks first, or else we forfeit our relationship with Him! But do explain that Jesus does not want us to "hate" our families (in Hebrew, "hate" is an idiom expressing lower priority among relationships).

Second, this passage also carries the demand for "reciprocal cross-bearing." We must also die!

As you manage the process, be aware—and explain if necessary—that this death of ours is (sometimes) not literal. Carefully listen to 2 Cor. 5:14-15:

> *For the love of Christ controls us, having concluded this, that one died for all, therefore all died; and He died for all, so that they who live might no longer live for themselves, but for Him who died and rose again on their behalf.*

A bond of love begins with Jesus dying sacrificially—and physically—for us on the Cross. Aware of this, we return His love with a sacrifice so total that it counts as our "death."

But Paul goes on to describe those who have *"died"* as *"they who live"*! If they died, how can they be described as living? The answer is that we die—not physically—but through self-denial. It is so complete that it results in us living for Jesus, instead of living for ourselves. We still have biological vital signs, however the self-sacrifice is so thorough and complete that it truly qualifies as dying! This explains how we can become *"living sacrifices"* (Romans 12:1)—sacrifice usually forces physical death. It also explains how we are able to *"die daily"* (1 Corinthians 15:31). Likewise, we can understand the enigmatic demand of Jesus for His follower to *"take up his cross daily"* (Luke 9:23)—actual crucifixion was absolutely non-repeatable! Jesus died physically, but we respond by daily yielding up our wills to Jesus. We bow to His Lordship. We have died.

Paul opened this amazing Scripture by pointing out the compelling power of the love of Jesus. That power—that love—has such force as to compel sinful people to completely surrender their lives to follow Jesus! That power energizes the covenant, the saving relationship. And, that power is outpoured when you set the gospel before a convert!

Decision Time!

You have brought your friend to the moment of decision! We have had a thorough discussion of Square Two, but don't worry—the actual work in our method is easy:

- First, insist that making the "saving relationship" work requires effort from both partners—human and Divine.
- Second, explain that God's contribution is giving us Jesus on the Cross (tell the story of the king rationing grain).
- Third, get agreement that we must respond by giving everything, as Jesus did for us (read Luke 9:23-27, then 9:57-62, then 14:25-27).

That's easy enough, right? Get the little "king story" down, with some practice. Read three Scriptures—all from Luke's Gospel and easily located five chapters apart.

You can do this!

Now, continue reading from where you are in Luke into 14:28-35. Read that passage aloud right now. Jesus never fails to amaze. He has set before His converts the biggest decision they ever will face: *"If anyone wishes to come after Me, he must deny himself, and take up his cross daily and follow Me."* In that day, everyone knew that "taking up your cross" meant just one thing: you are going to die!

The "magnitude of the step" that Jesus demands could not be more huge in terms of sacrifice! That's the decision demanded of us—take your place on a cross with Jesus, or walk away alone!

But Jesus knows the intense pressure we face. Rather than deciding cold and all at once, He first urges people to *"count the cost."* Give careful consideration to what Jesus offers in this proposal (salvation!). But also calculate carefully what He requires from you (everything!). After all, this is very serious. Is it really worth it? Decide well, because Jesus will not have room for any who are half-hearted, non-committal, and apt to back out later. *Take your time—as much time as you need to get this right!*

At this point, you should say:

> *"Jesus wants you to decide whether or not to follow Him. You need to "count the cost" for yourself. <u>You have as much time as you need</u>—whether that means five minutes, five years, or longer. But before you decide, you need to be absolutely sure. If you do decide to give your life to Jesus, let me know immediately. <u>Until that happens, we can go no further.</u>"*

Say this in your own words and offer a prayer for God's help.

In my experience, a very few will immediately decline the offer, and you will never hear back from them. To them, Jesus is not worth it. Sad, but some evaluate that way—and God allows this freedom of choice (yet there are consequences). Others may take extended time, and will call you when they are ready. However, many—or even most—will have already made up their minds and will be ready to proceed without delay. Only those who decide to respond to the Cross are ready for Square Three.

SQUARE THREE

Where we find SALVATION

"For God has not destined us for wrath, but for obtaining salvation through our Lord Jesus Christ, who died for us, so that whether we are awake or asleep, we will live together with Him."

—1 Thessalonians 5:9-10

"If there were more than one path to salvation then it would totally negate Jesus' sacrifice on the cross, his life, his teachings."

—Josh McDowell

If you arrive here, at Square Three, the hard work is done and over! You have brought someone and God together—both are agreed, both are ready for this. All that remains is something like a "wedding" to begin to the relationship.

The Cross is at the heart of that relationship and defines its shape. But God has set forth several requirements that give more clearly-defined shape. Think here of "wedding vows"—each one sets forth reasonable expectations for what the partnership must look like. It's important to spell some things out!

This is not a "checklist" that must be gotten out of the way to gain the prize!

These requirements are the "forever shapers" of a relationship with God that will soon begin and must retain that shape forever! We simply search the NT Scriptures for statements of every action required of people to receive salvation. I find only six of these—and each is vitally important:

Faith or Belief:

"For God so loved the world, that He gave His only begotten Son, that whoever believes in Him shall not perish, but have eternal life"

([John 3:16](#)). This is the essential requirement from which all others spring, and it carries dimensions of meaning—trust, belief, faithfulness, loyalty, relational trueness. Faith is continuing total allegiance to Jesus that mirrors what He did on the Cross. Faith is mutual, between God and us, creating a stable, reliable relationship.

Hearing The Word:

"So faith comes from hearing, and hearing by the word of Christ" ([Romans 10:17](#)). The faith that saves always is generated after we hear Biblical revelation from God. The Bible is the commonly held source of everyone's faith, and the relationship continues to be Biblical. It centers on "the word of Christ"—the gospel. No one gets to claim a private or mystical revelation. Even after conversion, reading the Bible allows us all to hear communication from God. Like faith, this communication is essential moving forward in relationship.

Spoken Confession of the Lordship of Jesus:

"that if you confess with your mouth Jesus as Lord, and believe in your heart that God

raised Him from the dead, you will be saved; for with the heart a person believes, resulting in righteousness, and with the mouth he confesses, resulting in salvation" (Romans 10:9-10). The word "confess" does not carry the usual meaning (to admit a failure). Here it means to say something out loud, with your voice, so as to claim a truth personally. To confess the Lordship of Jesus is to declare that He has consent to be your Lord or King, and that you consent to be a servant to Him. This requirement establishes the dynamic of authority. This requirement is equivalent to the one declared in the Great Commission: *"Go therefore and make disciples of all the nations...teaching them to observe all that I commanded you"* (Matthew 28:19-20).

Calling upon the Name of the Lord:

"For there is no distinction between Jew and Greek; for the same Lord is Lord of all, abounding in riches for all who call on Him; for 'WHOEVER WILL CALL ON THE NAME OF THE LORD WILL BE SAVED'" (Romans 10:12-13). Right from the beginning of this relationship, it is important to be open about the dynamic of dependence on Jesus. Salvation was not our idea; it was His! We did not take

the initiative; God did! Jesus did not need to be saved; we do! We call upon His Name (i.e. upon His authority) to find help and assistance in the salvation that only Jesus can provide.

Repentance:

"Repent, and each of you be baptized in the name of Jesus Christ for the forgiveness of your sins; and you will receive the gift of the Holy Spirit" (Acts 2:38). Repentance is "turning from" and "turning to"—a total reversal of direction. We turn away from the failure of a broken relationship with God and reorient ourselves to the reconciliation, the mending, the recovery that allows successful and healthy relating. The "turning from" is so drastic that it truly is a "death"—death to sin and death to self. Repentance brings the dynamic of holiness into the Christian experience with God. Our sinful and selfish life brought failure. So we leave it in the past because we have died to that kind of life to enter a holy life with God.

Baptism:

See again Acts 2:38 (quoted just above). Baptism is where we give ourselves over to die! Baptism is your death—your death that joins with the dying of Jesus on the Cross. Here, you take up your own cross! You have died for each other (giving your lives for each other counts as a "death"). You (as your "old self") go down into the water as though into a burial—and this death is permanent. Your "old self" never re-emerges. That person lived in sin, lived for self—good riddance!

In repentance, you made the determination to turn away from sin and to leave it behind as you now pursue a life of godly holiness. In this conversionary act, God gives you a new identity to replace the old; you are "born again" as you emerge from the baptismal waters. Your emergence from the watery grave finds oneness with the resurrection emergence of Jesus from the rich man's tomb. You have died with Jesus; you are also raised with Jesus.

Baptism joins the relationship between the convert and God. Like a wedding, baptism is a "covenant entrance ceremony" (Christianity and marriage are both "covenant" relationships). The action of baptism is immersion in water under God's authority or Name. The person immersed *had* no saving relationship with God. Through Jesus, the new person who emerges is now New-Covenant bound to God.

Baptism symbolizes a birth experience for a new child of God. God washes away the sins—however many and however great—from the convert, and he or she is then baptismally-born, pure and holy. The power that works this cleansing is the same power that resurrected Jesus.

Sins are washed away, resulting in salvation! The cleansing makes the body of the new Christian fit to be a dwelling place or "temple" for the Holy Spirit. In baptism, the Holy Spirit is placed inside the believer's heart to indwell there.

Your baptism shares much in common with the baptism of Jesus by John the Baptist—by this Jesus was "anointed" as the Christ/Messiah. Now you too are anointed! The Spirit brings holiness (or sanctification) into the believer's life with new power over sin.

Through baptism, the convert has a saving relationship with God through Jesus Christ—in other words, the convert is now a Christian!

Making This Manageable

We just covered a lot of information about the six requirements for salvation. Don't be overwhelmed or anxious. We will make this easy.

To begin with, churches of Christ have for long time used a "five-finger" memory hook: hear, believe, confess, repent, and be baptized. I complicate things by adding a sixth: calling upon the Name of the Lord. I recommend this preparation:

- <u>Memorize these on six fingers.</u> They need not be in order. However, "hearing" and "believing" are natural to begin the list, and "baptism" should come last as the climactic turning point at the end.
- You do not need to memorize the associated Scriptures. Write them down, or simply <u>memorize the locations, so you can find and read them.</u> There are only three locations that cover all six:

    —John 3:16 (believe)

    —three passages in Romans 10 (hear, confess, call upon the Name)

    —Acts 2:38 (repent, be baptized)

- You have memorized the six and can find supporting Scriptures. Work on learning how each "dynamic" will shape the relationship. Each will be as important in the resulting relationship as it was in the conversion:
    - Hearing the Word makes it Biblical
    - Believing (faith) makes it stable and reliable
    - Confessing establishes Jesus' authority as Lord
    - Calling upon the Name marks our dependence on Jesus
    - Repentance brings holiness
    - Baptism is where we die—and begin to live—with Jesus. Baptism is entrance into the covenant—like a wedding. Sins are removed and the Holy Spirit is received in the heart!

You can do this, right? You may need to jot this on a paper that you keep in your Bible. This is another area that gets easy with practice.

Just remember, there are only three things: (1) the six requirements, (2) the Scriptures, and (3) the relational dynamics.

The Finish

So, let's pick up where we left off. You are at Square Three when the convert has "counted the cost" and has decided that relationship is worth the sacrifice of everything. I usually feel compelled to raise a prayer of thanks, first for the salvation Jesus brings by His Cross and second for the convert's decision to enter the relationship that brings salvation. Then I say,

> *"Remember that we said that a Christian is someone who has a "saving relationship" with God through Jesus? Now we need to find what makes for a "saving" relationship. You know, it is true that everyone has a relationship with God (however, most people have a bad or failing relationship with God). We are interested in finding a "saving" relationship—and to find out what that is, I have gone through the New Testament Scriptures of the Bible to find everything that God says we must do to be saved."*

I lead the convert through the list of six requirements, reading the Scripture supporting each one. Then, describe how doing each of these things creates the relationship that God wants to have with us—and therefore He rewards that relationship with salvation. As appropriate, I make the requirements personal, making sure that the convert knows what is required and is willing to comply and obey God. Obvious sins that need to end through repentance may not be so obvious to the convert. Anyone willing to die for Jesus will easily accept these demands as reasonable. The last requirement is baptism.

When it comes to baptism, I attempt by all means to do this immediately. *Tomorrow may be too late; the time for delay was while "counting the cost"!* There should now be eagerness with the convert—as there is with God—to enter the relationship. As I see it, a romantic couple should take their good time before making the big decision to marry—that is a decision of great magnitude! But once they are so engaged, they should act quickly to wed! Why would a convert delay baptism after responding to the gospel?

I like to gather the church members for the event, but always ask first for the convert's consent. I also ask what others he or she may wish to invite to be present. Some prefer a crowd; others prefer privacy. While I offer to perform the baptism myself, there may be spiritual or merely personal reasons to prefer a different baptizer. The convert may make these decisions.

This may be your first success at evangelism, and so it may be your first time to perform a baptism! You may wonder how to do this? First, discuss the mechanics. He or she will hold their nose to keep water out. With one arm behind his back, with the other hand you grasp the forearm that holds the nose. The convert will lean backward until entirely under the water. Agree that readiness to go under should be signaled with a nod of the head. Promise to quickly raise them out of the water!

Just before baptism, often while standing in the water, I give opportunity to vocalize confession of Jesus' Lordship. Often, with the model of Acts 8:37, we simply ask, *"Do you believe that Jesus is the Son of God?"* This suggests acceptance of Jesus' authority and all that needs to be said is, *"I do!"* What happens consciously during baptism is very important. I counsel the person—*while under the waters, alone with God*—to focus on just two thoughts:

- That Jesus, on the Cross, gave everything for me!
- That I—now taking up my own cross—give everything for Jesus!

GETTING TO SQUARE ONE

How to Find a Convert

"Conduct yourselves with wisdom toward outsiders, making the most of the opportunity. Let your speech always be with grace, as though seasoned with salt, so that you will know how you should respond to each person."

—Colossians 4:5-6

"Jesus himself did not try to convert the two thieves on the cross; he waited until one of them turned to him."

—Dietrich Bonhoeffer

This is the hard part! I have repeatedly told you that the Three Squares method is easy. It is, once you have someone ready to listen to the gospel of Jesus.

And there's the rub....

Everyone needs salvation. But not everyone you meet will be spiritually receptive. However carefully we do our work to bond them to a relationship with Jesus, each convert embarks on one of the four trajectories set forth in the Parable of the Sower (Mark 4:1-20):

- Some will fall to Satan even before sprouting.
- Some will sprout, then quickly wilt.
- Some will get further, but spiritual life gets choked out by worldly forces.
- Others will reach the harvest in full reproductive maturity.

Forces beyond your control will bring failure or success. Your job is not to find people, whose success is guaranteed before you are willing to share the gospel. Prepare yourself—some of your work will end in failure. Be willing to put effort into people who show little hope for success. Jesus is mighty to save!

However, give nothing to those who are openly defiant and blasphemous toward God and all that is holy. Jesus warned: *"Do not give what is holy to dogs, and do not throw your pearls before swine, or they will trample them under their feet, and turn and tear you to pieces"* (Matt. 7:6). Instead of sharing the gospel with profane "trolls," if you are bold enough, give them a warning!

In days when I was hostile and resisted conversion, a friend declared: *"John, I've told you about Jesus and I can see you don't care. Just remember this: when you face Jesus at the Final Judgment, you can no longer claim that you didn't know any better!"* Outwardly, I didn't even flinch. Inwardly, fear shot through my heart and I carried that fear like burning-hot coals for three years! That warning had a good effect. It helped give me "ears to hear" when another person shared the gospel with me much later.

This Is War!

God and Satan are at war—and all of us are caught in the middle! Each of us, by sinning, joined rebellion against God. Evangelistic conversion changes our allegiance and we again side with God. We work to bring others with us, while the devil works to hold them.

If you want to win some battles, make sure your own "saving relationship" with God is lively and active! Be nourished on words of Scripture; lift up prayers; love God strongly and constantly; shun sin and live in holiness; keep faith. Walk in relationship with God, and He will be your power and fight your battles. Otherwise, you are on your own (Acts 17:13-16).

Evangelism is truly supernatural! You will actively engage forces that are both Divine and anti-God. Working powerfully through you, in profound wisdom that is not your own, God will win victories and the baptismal waters will stir!

Introverts and Extroverts

God can use all of us. I am an introvert, which means I find inner strength when I am alone. Some of you are extroverts, and you feel stronger in company with others. It is uncomfortable for me to take chances socially and face the risk of rejection; some of us find social play exciting and fun. Some of us can stand in the check-out line in a store and, right there, share the gospel with a perfect stranger. Others will find that awkward and frightening. In general, it is easier for an extrovert to "tone it down" than it is for the introvert to expand the "comfort zone." In certain situations, even an introvert may open up and find courage to share the good news of Jesus.

All of us face the temptation to say nothing when we should speak up for Jesus. And to both introverts and to extroverts (right after discussing self-denial and taking up one's cross to follow Him), Jesus declares: *"...whoever is ashamed of Me and My words in this adulterous and sinful generation, the Son of Man will also be ashamed of him when He comes in the glory of His Father with the holy angels"* (Mark 8:38).

Evangelism is NOT only for those who can do it comfortably and are brimming with confidence! It is also a God-given responsibility for those with wild heart palpitations during an adrenaline rush!

Those with natural social courage and with the charisma to draw strangers to Square One should act accordingly for the gospel. You may be one who "has never met a stranger." You have inner courage to take chances and to be quite bold, even with strangers! Do what comes naturally: engage, invite, mingle, outreach. Extroverts will do this easily and naturally.

Introverts are a different matter, but here is a suggestion that might work. It finds support in Luke 10:5, where Jesus gives instructions to pairs of disciples sent out to preach. They are to extend a greeting to a house. Then, depending on reception or rejection, they either bless the house (with a visit) or depart (after a warning or curse). The strategy: *put something out, and then watch.* Put out a simple remark that is "spiritual"—perhaps something about morality or religion:

- "I heard of a study suggesting Christian marriages are happier."
- "Did you hear of the suicide of a popular actor or athlete?"
- "Why do you think young people lose hope so easily?"

The key is to watch the response for a sign that it is socially "safe" to advance such a discussion (introverts avoid unsafe interactions). If you find interest and engagement, quickly follow with another remark. It's like feeding a baby: as long there is eagerness—

and the mouth opens for more—keep spooning! But, if the beets or spinach are blubbering down the chin—rather than being swallowed—back off! Eventually, the conversation may lead to Square One and you sense the opportunity to ask, *"What is a Christian?"*

Introverts may find it more comfortable and natural to take a cautious and careful approach, but they can still get to Square One with a good strategy.

Another suggestion is for extroverts and introverts to team-up and work together. Jesus liked to send His people out in pairings. There are advantages to supportive cooperation. Sometimes the one with social skills can get a prospect to Square One, and then even the more shy partner can finish the conversion. Christian marriages make natural evangelistic pairings. They say "opposites attract." The natural socialite may compensate for the quiet spouse. Likewise in ministry, even an introverted preacher is capable of evangelistically finishing the social leads fed to him by other Christians. God has arranged the members of the church for strategic success (1 Corinthians 12:18).

We should all find it easier to reach Square One by tapping existing social networks—

friends, neighbors, co-workers, etc. Many of them may not get another evangelistic opportunity unless you provide it.

Just as many use these already established relationships to peddle merchandise for profit, these same relationships may be exploited to glorify Jesus (ponder the enigmatic parable in Luke 16:1-9). However, Christians should never drive relationships both toward evangelism (God's business) and also to marketing merchandise (your business)! Listen to Paul as he speaks for God: *"For we are not like many, peddling the word of God, but as from sincerity, but as from God, we speak in Christ in the sight of God"* (2 Corinthians 2:17, NASB).

Do not attempt to make a sale before, during, or after sharing the gospel! The convert will sense your efforts to be sheer manipulation for your own benefit while you "peddle the word of God." There are plenty of religious hucksters working gullible yet good-hearted people for their own profit, while turning them forever against God! Evangelism is holy business—God's business! And you cannot serve both God and money (Luke 16:13).

One more suggestion: <u>ride the wave of evangelistic success.</u> Each convert you win to Jesus opens the door to a new social network. Often, people will come around with curiosity to try to understand the cause to which a friend has made a life-altering commitment. My wife and I became Christians in wave fashion. My best friend's life was completely changed by Jesus, and we were worried! We suspected he had been brainwashed by a cult and went to rescue him. That put us at Square One!

SIMPLE OUTLINE OF METHOD

Here you will find the method stripped to its basic and essential form. Although it is quite simple, you should prepare yourself to work it effectively and with confidence. A listing of necessary preparations follows the outline.

SQUARE ONE: where we find FOCUS!

THE QUESTION: *"What is a Christian?"*

ANSWER: a person who has a saving relationship with God through Jesus Christ.

The convert is asked to answer the Question. Unless we receive the correct answer, our typical response is: *"While that is something that a Christian DOES, it doesn't tell us what a Christian IS. Try again?"* Repeat to the point of exasperation!

SQUARE TWO: where we find POWER!

Every relationship, to be successful, requires contributions from both partners.

God's contribution to relationship: the life of Jesus on the Cross! (Illustration: story of king rationing grain.)

Our obligatory responsive contribution: our life given in total sacrifice!

> Read Luke 9:23-27; 57-62—total self-sacrifice: deny self, take up cross! Jesus must win any "competition among relationships." Read Luke 14:25-27.

Counting the cost: continue reading into Luke 14:28-35. Announce that it is now decision time. The convert must decide whether Jesus is worth such sacrifice, and the process must come to a halt to allow "cost counting"—however much time that requires.

The Cross demands response, and the only worthy response is to answer the total self-sacrifice of Jesus with our responsive total self-sacrifice. Four readings from Luke clarify this and finally lead to a "cost counting" decision. The evangelistic process is halted indefinitely and cannot resume until decision is reached.

SQUARE THREE: where we find SALVATION!

The "saving relationship" is further defined by every NT requirement for salvation:

- Faith from hearing God's Word (John 3:16; Romans 10:17)
- Spoken "confession" of the Lordship of Jesus and calling on the Name of the Lord (Romans 10:9-13)
- Repentance and baptism (Acts 2:38)

State the goal of searching the entire NT for every "salvation" requirement. Read relevant Scriptures and explain how each gives a special shape or quality to our relationship with Jesus, and is therefore necessary. Explain baptism as the place where dying with Jesus becomes real—it is a death to self and a death to sin as Jesus becomes our Lord. We are saved as our sins are forgiven and as the Spirit is given to us. Explain that, following baptism, we must strive for sinless living and that the Holy Spirit will empower us. Ask that, while under the water, the only thought is: Jesus gave His live for me and now I give my life for Him!

PREPARING FOR SUCCESS

For SQUARE ONE: Practice the question-and-answer: *"What is a Christian?"* Do this with live people until you feel confident.

For SQUARE TWO: Practice telling the "king story." Be sure to say it out loud until you can tell it meaningfully and can apply its meaning to explain what Jesus did for us on the Cross and why our sin made it necessary.

For SQUARE THREE: The needed information may be retrieved either from memory or from a "cheat sheet" kept in the Bible. Memorize the six "forever shapers" of the relationship with God: hearing the Word, belief or faith, repentance, confessing the Lordship of Jesus, calling upon His Name, and baptism. Memorize the three Scripture locations that spell out the requirement for all six "forever shapers." Memorize the quality or characteristic that each "forever shaper" brings to shape the saving relationship (for example, repentance makes for a "holy" relationship).

SQUARE THREE is the most demanding because we transfer a lot of info. Take comfort that the hard work was already done. The convert has counted the cost and is agreeable to fully obey. Now you must finish this! Determine to learn the material so as to be able to communicate it.

WHY A "SAVING RELATIONSHIP"?

Read the Bible, cover to cover, and God is yearning, working, strategizing over long stretches of time to engage people in successful relationship. His effort and heart are amazing; our God is a lover of people. He nurtures, sends gifts (blessings), instructs, and perfectly models truthfulness, enduring loyalty, and warmest love. If that doesn't work, God punishes, threatens, and even condemns. If even that fails to make for relational success, God sends His Son to take our failures from us. We are given a start-over, many times—as many as it takes. Still not enough? God sends His Spirit and places Him in our hearts to provide us with extra power to do relationship right.

People, on the other hand? We fail relationships. The Bible calls this failure "sin," and we are so easily and readily prone to it that it looks like we were born for failure: *"For man is born for trouble, as sparks fly upward"* (Job 5:7). God wrote that—and He has lots of experience to draw from. We are easily corrupted by selfishness and dishonesty. If that doesn't work, we dissolve interpersonal bonds of trust and loyalty. Still not enough? We have more ways of using words and deeds than can be counted to hurt others. We simply are not good at relationships. We are good at being bad at relationships!

Our need for saving relationship with God could not be more obvious.

Right Religion? The evangelistic method of this book drives toward right relationship. This could be challenged. Is this really the true target and goal? Why not aim instead at right religion?

Because God has shown us in His Book that even those who get religion right can still be relational failures (sinners). One may be physically "circumcised" in obedience to God without being "circumcised in heart." You can get into the right religion and still be a failure. Religious purity has led people to carefully weigh-out garden herbs to give God a proper sacrifice. But you can do that, yet fail to develop relational essentials like fairness, fervent love, and faithfulness (Matthew 23:23). And Christian religionists are as prone to failure as were the Jewish. Jesus saw that coming:

Not everyone who says to Me, "Lord, Lord," will enter the kingdom of heaven, but he who does the will of My Father who is in heaven will enter. Many will say to Me on that day, "Lord, Lord, did we not prophesy in Your name, and in Your name cast out demons, and in Your name perform many miracles?" And then I will declare to them, "I never knew you; DEPART FROM ME, YOU WHO PRACTICE LAWLESSNESS" (Matthew 7:21-23).

Here, Jesus marks out people with the hallmarks of Christian religion:

- They call Jesus not only *"Lord,"* but *"Lord, Lord."*
- They have sided against Satan, exorcising demons.
- They are spiritually gifted to prophesy and work miracles.

All this going for them, and yet Jesus casts them out (much as they had cast out demons). Why? Jesus speaks in terms of relationship: *"I never knew you!"* That one relational negative outweighs all the religious positives. Truth is, not everyone sitting inside the right church in the right religion has a right relationship with God!

Right Belief? This is the aim of "easy believe-ism." The essentiality of faith is sometimes expressed in the Bible as though nothing else matters. And, to hear some people tell it, the only Scripture necessary for salvation is: *"For God so loved the world, that He gave His only begotten Son, that whoever believes in Him shall not perish, but have eternal life"* (John 3:16). Simply believe that Jesus came and died to change your final destination from Hell to Heaven! Just believe those few facts and salvation is yours—easy!

Why do we value correct beliefs? We are children of the Age of Science. Science has driven us to determine factuality before we "believe" something. We divide categories of science and superstition—true and false, right and wrong, fact and fiction, history and mythology. The claims of Christianity are subjected to evaluation—those who "believe" are Christians, and they get salvation solely on the basis of believing the factual reality about Jesus—easy!

However, faith (or belief) has several other dimensions of meaning. That is why the original Greek words are translated into so many different English words: belief or believing, faith, trust, faithfulness or loyalty. The ancient people were concerned about scientific and historical factuality (and back then, as in our day, many fools were superstitious). *But the greater concerns about "faith" (or belief) are always relational—and that is not easy!*

In relationship, partners may "believe in" each other—or, they may not! Partners may "be true" to each other—and a scientist is not needed to determine that! Loyalty and faithfulness are the "facts" of relationship.

Now both "factuality" and "relational qualities" are necessary for Biblical faith—for faith that brings salvation. To turn in faith from false gods to the true God is a concern of reality, or ontology, or epistemology. But after this determination, what sort of relationship will be entered with the one true God—faithful or faithless? Easy believe-ism does not extend the essential scope of faith to include relational concerns, and therefore is not true to the Bible witness. *Faith that does not achieve relational success does not achieve salvation:*

> *"You believe that God is one. You do well; the demons also believe, and shudder"* (James 2:19, NASB).

Yes, the demons knew the facts, and "believed." But they get no salvation, which made them shudder with terror! Why? Because the faith that saves is not merely factual; it is relational!

Right Morals? This is similar to right religion. Some claim a right standing before God, and a right to salvation, for being a "good person," for having a moral code to live by. This seems reasonable, especially if you compare yourself against really bad people (like Hitler, or serial killers). But is God looking for nothing more than people who live cleanly, who have an active conscience, and who abide by a code of morality?

If you believe this, then you need to read Mark 10:17-31. Jesus encounters a man who lived successfully by the moral code written by God—the Ten Commandments. *"Looking at him, Jesus felt a love for him and said to him, 'One thing you lack: go and sell all you possess and give to the poor, and you will have treasure in heaven; and come, follow Me.'"* (vs. 21). Nothing but a vital relationship would prompt a wealthy man to give it all up, and relationship was the one thing he lacked! But he was a moral rule-keeper—wasn't that enough? According to Jesus, no. The man approached with a question about what one needed to inherit eternal life and left empty.

Right religion, right belief, right morals—all so right; all so important. But being right in these vital ways will bring salvation only if one has a "right relationship" with God through Christ Jesus!

More Support for a Relational Focus

Strictly speaking, the Bible is not a book about God; it also says a lot about people. Really the Bible sets focus on relationship between God and people! And, that makes sense since Jesus tied the two greatest commandments (Matthew 22:36-40) to relational functioning (which is what "love" is all about):

> *One of them, a lawyer, asked Him a question, testing Him, "Teacher, which is the great commandment in the Law?"*

> *And He said to him, "'YOU SHALL LOVE THE LORD YOUR GOD WITH ALL YOUR HEART, AND WITH ALL YOUR SOUL, AND WITH ALL YOUR MIND.' This is the great and foremost commandment. The second is like it, 'YOU SHALL LOVE YOUR NEIGHBOR AS YOURSELF.' On these two commandments depend the whole Law and the Prophets."*

Some relationships that are essential to understanding God's Book involve entire groups of people—they are called the "covenants." The Old Testament Scriptures featured the Jewish nation of Israel under the Old Covenant which was mediated through Moses. As expressed in the New Testament Scriptures, Jesus mediates the New Covenant, first with Jews and later expanded to include Christians of all nations. The Old and New covenants together were advancing the larger purpose of God through the covenant with Abraham. Although it originated with the one man, Abraham, its aim was universal to all humanity.

To fully understand the Bible, these supra-relationships—along with the covenants of Noah and David—are essential mechanisms that drive the plot that aims at successful relationship between people and God. Driven by this meaning, it only makes sense to see "relationship" as the pure essence of Christianity, as core to becoming a Christian.

The method of evangelism of this book aims at a saving relationship with God through Christ Jesus. The Bible is witness that this aim is true.

WHAT IS COVENANT?

There are many forms that relationship may take—neighbor, friendship, business partner, citizenship, romantic, etc. One particular form of relationship is called "covenant."

The two partners in covenant begin by pledging themselves together in unending loyalty and unfailing love. Then, they watch each other with "eagle eyes" for signs in behavior that this pledge is honored or dishonored. Words are important, but actions more so. Any violation of a relational obligation is called "sin." In an honored covenant, the faithful partner is rewarded with "blessings." A sinful partner in covenant, however, comes under "curses" as punishment. Covenants are very conditional relationships because the quality of relating determines success or failure. It takes two contributing partners to guarantee success.

Covenants are enforced by God. He listens as witness when covenantal vows, pledges, or promises are exchanged—not only for relationships between two people, but also in those in which one partner is God himself. God cares about how people treat one another, and also about honoring covenants in which He is partnered directly. Each of the Two Greatest Commandments (Matthew 22:36-40) attests to God's oversight over all relationships.

All covenants with at least one human partner will experience failure (sin). Some sins are so egregious, and are so damaging to the essence and foundation of the relationship, that they break it. The partnership dissolves because the basis for trust has been removed; promises have been broken. However, not all sins are fatal to a covenant. Covenants are remedial; their strained integrity may be restored as one partner "repents" and the other extends forgiving "grace." Reconciliation brings covenant renewal.

God has provided a "learning tool" to make sure we all can understand covenant-relating: marriage. Marriage between husband and wife is a covenant (Ephesians 5:21ff.)! Since marriage is the core relationship within any and every culture, it may be observed by all for learning and instruction. Whoever understands marriage—and the dynamics that bring success or failure—thereby understands covenant. God forgives His partners in much the same way as do spouses. Like them, God deeply cares about the quality or "truth" of the relationship.

The goal of evangelism presented here is a New Covenant Relationship between every Christian and God, through Jesus. The essence of it: the sacrifice of Jesus (as Sin-bearer) on the Cross answered by the self-sacrifice of sinners who "take up their own crosses." *The New Covenant is a Life given for a life!* It is total devotion and love without limit in reciprocal exchange.

Obviously, God is able to relate with perfection; His love and faithfulness are flawless. We who are human covenant-partners fail to lesser or greater degrees. Covenants show their value here, because these relationships excel at coupling partners who differ: husbands and wives; masters and slaves; Divine and human; sinful and Sinless. Grace and forgiveness are essentials in a covenant.

However, the New Covenant not only forgives sins, it prevents them. Jewish partners in the Old Covenant stood before relational obligations to God with only the natural strength and ability known to humans. Predictably they failed; often and terribly. This natural state is called "living by the flesh"—the problem is not that "the flesh" is inherently evil, but rather that it is weak.

Paul describes this well in Romans 7. Under the Old Covenant, the Jewish people of God had the Law from God but could not keep it. This failure—while living "in the flesh"—was experienced even when the desire to obey God was sincere and strong. The will was there; the ability to do it was not! Living "by the flesh" means using your own moral and spiritual strength. Old Covenant experience has proven that the flesh is insufficient. It lacks the strength.

The New Covenant experience is described in Romans 8 (but not in Chapter 7!). Christians, in covenant with God through Jesus, are given a power source: the indwelling Holy Spirit. Faced with the challenge to obey God, the Christian has the same "fleshly" strength as everyone else—and then some! Faced with temptations to sin, the Christian has the same "fleshly" strength as everyone else—and then some! This strength is supernatural and comes to us from an outside Source. Sins that would have been committed are avoided by Spirit-filled Christians under the New Covenant.

This extra power was seen in Jesus. The embrace of Spirit by Jesus owes itself to His baptism, which marks the beginning of His messianic ministry. For some thirty years prior, Jesus lived a rather ordinary life. But His baptism by John, marked by Heavenly Voice and Descending Spirit, touches off a three-year frenzy of Spirit-fueled activity and words. The Christ has now been anointed (Luke 4:18; Acts 10:38)! When you were baptized, you also received the Holy Spirit. He dwells in your heart and brings power that you never had while living "in the flesh"!

I do not want to leave the impression that "living by the flesh" was a problem only for Jewish believers under the Old Covenant. That specific failure is presented as characteristic and is highlighted and underscored to make this rhetorical point: Christians—don't you permit yourself to fall back into spiritual weakness and, thus, into a failed relationship with God! How could you allow that, when God has afforded you spiritual strength and power through His gift to you of the Holy Spirit? That Spirit is—right now—dwelling in your heart! God's presence is with you directly, personally, and constantly. You are the new Temple! How dare you now live in the fleshly ways common to unconverted humanity? We might have expected such failure pre-conversion, but not post-conversion (1 Corinthians 6:9-11). Paul addresses "fleshly" failure among Christians in several places, but see especially 1 Cor. 2:6-3:3. Here Paul speaks to Christians who are "living by the flesh":

> *And I, brethren, could not speak to you as to spiritual men, but as to men of flesh, as to infants in Christ. I gave you milk to drink, not solid food; for you were not yet able to receive it. Indeed, even now you are not yet able, for you are still fleshly. For since there is jealousy and strife among you, are you not fleshly, and are you not walking like mere men?*

See also in Galatians the battle—within the church fellowship—between the anti-spiritualities "of flesh" and "of Spirit." The spirituality properly characteristic of Christianity generates the "fruit of the Spirit"; while Christians who continue in the weak, infantile failings (that historically were characteristic of Jewish believers) generate the "works of the flesh" (read all of Galatians 5). Christians are also capable of living by the flesh!

Covenant with God is a powerful relationship.

THE MAGNITUDE OF THE STEP

"According to the grace of God which was given to me, like a wise master builder I laid a foundation, and another is building on it. But each man must be careful how he builds on it."

—1 Corinthians 3:10, NASB

Everyone takes a step to complete their conversion. For some it's a small step. For others, it is a step of greatest magnitude. The magnitude required depends largely on the demands set forth by the evangelist—some make it tough to become a Christian; other ministers make it as easy as possible. There is great variability and that raises the question: what magnitude of step does the Lord Jesus require for one to enter a saving relationship?

True story. During a gospel-meeting campaign, a teenage girl asked to be baptized.

The preaching-school student who attended to her conversion asked about her sins because part of the "step" requires repentance. She stated she had no awareness of any sins. Then why, he asked, did she want to be baptized at all? She replied, *"There is so much love in this church that I want to be part of this family!"* He shared the story and explained his decision to baptize her: *"I can't see how God could object to that, so neither do I."* That is a very small step to take.

My failure. When I worked my earliest evangelisms, I knew baptism resulted in salvation. So I would set before my converts the "five-finger checklist" of salvation requirements: hear, believe, confess, repent, and be baptized. *"Do that,"* I said confidently, *"and salvation is yours!"* When the resulting baptisms were done and over, I had not yet spoken a single word about the Cross. I had not shared the gospel. Small wonder I was able to find some willing to take such a tiny step for such a spectacular prize. My bad!

A cartoon. In a single frame, we see two couples sitting on living room furniture with Bibles open on their laps. Their facial expressions display an incredulous lack of words adequate to respond to the woman who blurts out: *"Well, I never actually DIED to sin—but I did feel kind of faint once!"* Ouch! You are with me if you wonder if that poor woman's conversion was deficient.

It is not my interest here to be the one who judges between true and false Christians based on the adequacy of their conversions. That role belongs only to the Lord Jesus. But, if you will bear with me, I would like to speak in a cautionary way to readers who will work conversions and want to do that work competently.

The Magnitude Jesus Demands

TOTAL SURRENDER. *"The kingdom of heaven is like a treasure hidden in the field, which a man found and hid again; and from joy over it he goes and sells all that he has and buys that field. Again, the kingdom of heaven is like a merchant seeking fine pearls, and upon finding one pearl of great value, he went and sold all that he had and bought it"* (Matt. 13:44-46).

Those admitted to the kingdom sacrifice all self-interest for Jesus—He is the treasure, the pearl worth any sacrifice. They approach with that willingness. I remember reading Juan Carlos Ortiz years ago. He imagined

Jesus and a convert/follower coming to terms. Jesus asked what he owned, and to every possession named, Jesus declared, *"I'll take that now!"*—wealth, home, even family members. Is that price too steep? Is the magnitude too great? Jesus does not think so. He demands everything from those who want Him!

Some might prefer an easier and smaller step. Listen to Wilbur Rees: *"I would like to buy $3 worth of God, please. Not enough to explode my soul or disturb my sleep, but just enough to equal a cup of warm milk or a snooze in the sunshine. I don't want enough of God to make me love my enemies or pick beets with a migrant. I want ecstasy, not transformation. I want the warmth of the womb, not a new birth. I want a pound of the Eternal in a paper sack. I would like to buy $3 worth of God, please."*

NO COMPETITION BETWEEN RELATIONSHIPS. *"If anyone comes to Me, and does not hate his own father and mother and wife and children and brothers and sisters, yes, and even his own life, he cannot be My disciple"* (Luke 14:26). We may soften this a bit by admitting that Hebrew idiom uses "hate," not literally, but to express lower priority among relationships. Jacob was said to "hate" Leah—but look how many children he fathered by her! We need not hate our families to be Christians. However, Jesus demands that relationship with Him wins against competing interests in any other relationship!

A SECOND CROSS. *"And He was saying to them all, 'If anyone wishes to come after Me, he must deny himself, and take up his cross <u>daily</u> and follow Me'"* (Luke 9:23). The gospel that saves does not have a single Cross; it has two. One of them belongs to you. Everyone in that day knew that taking up your cross meant just one thing: you are going to die! That may actually mean the physical death of a martyr (Rev. 2:10). That would not be an unreasonable sacrifice for a Savior who takes a Cross himself for you.

But the word "daily" tips us off to another possible meaning (cf. 1 Cor. 15:31). It means a self-sacrifice so thorough that it virtually is a death: *"For the love of Christ controls us, having concluded this, that one died for all, therefore all died; and He died for all, so that they who live might no longer live for themselves, but for Him who died and rose again on their behalf"* (2 Cor. 5:14-15). Strange concept indeed, but there is such a thing as a *"living sacrifice"* (Rom.12:1).

None of these huge steps are optional. None are presented as long-range goals for a Christian to reach after steady spiritual growth and maturation. They are conversionary prerequisites, or one is not accepted by Jesus.

Towards Robust Baptism

Not only is the magnitude of the step often eased as a requirement. Baptism likewise gets the stuffing pulled out, until only a shadow of itself remains.

Baptism is the conversionary act of getting-wet-all-over plus a stuffing of many inherent meanings: remission of sins (Acts 2:38; 22:16), salvation (Mark 16:16; 1 Peter 3:21); enrollment in church membership (Acts 2:41; 1 Cor. 12:13), reception of the Holy Spirit (Acts 2:38; 19:2-3), and dying with Jesus (Rom. 6:3-4). I am sure this list is not exhaustive.

The question arises: what if someone gets-wet-all-over while ignorant of some or all of these meanings? Is the baptism still valid? Will God fulfill all such meanings and allow the convert to learn of them later? What if someone had no awareness of dying with Jesus; would that happen regardless?

I have heard hypotheticals played out until the only essential requirement left to a stripped-down baptism was obeying the act of getting-wet-all-over in response to God's command. The "obedience" itself yielded efficacy—apart from any attached meaning(s). Listen, I am not getting cheeky or being flippant when I refer to baptism as getting-wet-all-over. But getting-wet-all-over is all that remains if the stuffing is all pulled out of this conversionary act. And that is precisely the aspect of baptism marked out by 1 Peter 3:21 as inconsequential for achieving salvation—*"not the removal of dirt from the flesh."* Yes, immersion in water is essential, but the real action takes place in the *"conscience"*—and for that to be possible we need a more robust understanding of what baptism means.

It is not my intent to spell out what the essential meanings of baptism are. It is not my intent to deny the validity of any baptism that has some ignorance of theological meaning. Perhaps some meaning can be learned after the fact, after the act. That may be possible. But I do know that Paul asked, *"Or do you not know that all of us who have been baptized into Christ Jesus have been baptized into His death?"* And he asked this in such way that indicates confidence that the Roman church had at least that much stuffing in their baptisms. But the point that I wish to make is this: some of the stuffing needs to be inside of baptism for the act to function as a conversionary requirement—and the more the better. Let's move toward robust baptism!

Be a Wise Master Builder!

"According to the grace of God which was given to me, like a wise master builder I laid a foundation, and another is building on it. But each man must be careful how he builds on it. For no man can lay a foundation other than the one which is laid, which is Jesus Christ. Now if any man builds on the foundation with gold, silver, precious stones, wood, hay, straw, each man's work will become evident; for the day will show it because it is to be revealed with fire, and the fire itself will test the quality of each man's work. If any man's work which he has built on

it remains, he will receive a reward. If any man's work is burned up, he will suffer loss; but he himself will be saved, yet so as through fire. Do you not know that you are a temple of God and that the Spirit of God dwells in you? If any man destroys the temple of God, God will destroy him, for the temple of God is holy, and that is what you are" (1 Cor. 3:10-17).

This Scripture is concerned with the quality of convert brought into our circle of fellowship through evangelistic process. Two factors are determinative. Each one baptized launches into one of four trajectories set forth in the Parable of the Sower. Three of these fall to failure. The quality and competence of the evangelist's work will show, but even the best workmanship cannot prevent all failure. Some work will be *"burned up"* anyway. The convert also has responsibility for his own success, for the length of his trajectory.

The evangelist, however, is largely responsible. If his convert is lost and has himself to blame, all that the preacher has worked for with that particular person will be lost forever. But the preacher will survive spiritually—

apparently because some matters were out of his hands. Yet, he—based on the quality of his workmanship—also will have to pass through the fires of Divine judgment. If he is to be saved, God will have to sort out responsibility between converter and convert.

What is critical is that conversionary building rests upon the one foundation: Jesus Christ. And again I ask: what magnitude of step lands one atop that foundation? How robustly full of Scriptural meaning must baptism be to launch a trajectory that takes seed to harvest? Be careful how you build!

I have shown you how to do this in this book. The method is simple and undemanding on you; but your converts will need to take a step of greatest magnitude!

OBEYING THE GOSPEL

*"...dealing out retribution to those who do not know God and to those who **do not obey the gospel** of our Lord Jesus."*

—2 Thessalonians 1:8 (NASB)

*"For it is time for judgment to begin with the household of God; and if it begins with us first, what will be the outcome for those who **do not obey the gospel** of God?"*

—1 Peter 4:17 (NASB)

Paul agrees with Peter; Peter with Paul—failure to "obey the gospel" is fatal! But what is "the gospel"? And how does one obey that?

The gospel is the event (it is simultaneously the message of that event) which centers on the Cross-death of Jesus, His burial in a tomb, His rising to full resurrection-life, and His appearances alive-after-death to eyewitnesses. Listen to Paul (1 Corinthians 15:1-5, NASB):

> *Now I make known to you, brethren, <u>the gospel</u> which I preached to you, which also you received, in which also you stand, by which also you are saved, if you hold fast the word which I preached to you, unless you believed in vain. For I delivered to you as of first importance what I also received, that <u>Christ died</u> for our sins according to the Scriptures, and that <u>He was buried</u>, and that <u>He was raised</u> on the third day according to the Scriptures, and that <u>He appeared</u>....*

The gospel is an event, albeit a complex event—death, burial, raising, appearances. The gospel begins with—and centers on—the crucifixion of Jesus. *But how would you "obey" Someone's death?*

The obvious answer is that you "obey" the death of Jesus by answering with a death of your own (in terms of a full self-sacrifice)! You answer His Cross by denying yourself and taking up your own cross to follow Jesus (Luke 9:23)! To obey the gospel, you are *"crucified with Christ"* (Gal. 2:20). That has been the consistent theology beneath this book and the method of evangelism that it generates.

A Shared Cross-Death Experience

The gospel event is the working of God to create relationship with sinful human converts! Relationship thus forms between God and people "through Jesus Christ." It is a saving relationship, which explains why the literal meaning of the Greek word for "gospel" is "good news"! The essence of this relationship is the reciprocal self-sacrifice—a shared cross-death experience—between Jesus and someone else. This is correct theology—it must be gotten right for any conversion experience to be valid and true to Scripture. This is what it means to "obey the gospel"!

This "two-cross exchange" is the essence of the relationship that is called the "New Covenant" in NT Scripture. The phrase *"forgiveness (or remission) of sins"* links together the two crosses in the New Covenant—the Cross-death of Jesus with the baptismal cross-death of the convert. Listen first to Jesus: *"...for this is My blood of the covenant, which is poured out for many for forgiveness of sins"* (Matthew 26:28). Compare Peter's use of the identical phrase when he commands converts to be baptized: *"Repent, and each of you be baptized in the name of Jesus Christ for the forgiveness of your sins; and you will receive the gift of the Holy Spirit"* (Acts 2:38). The link between Cross and baptism is one of relationship, of covenant. Obeying the gospel is thus equivalent to entering the New Covenant and sins are forgiven.

Carefully follow me here. *Obeying the gospel requires TWO deaths, which finally morph together into a shared death-experience.* Jesus' death on the Cross is obvious—that is one of the essential deaths. Then, in baptism, the believer experiences the second death of his "old self" (Rom. 6:6), which is signified by funeral-like burial in water. It is thus a death to self.

The "self" had ever been the authority figure—the ruler who sat upon the throne of the heart. But before baptism, the believer *"confessed Jesus as Lord"* (Rom. 10:9-10). The self is now dethroned! Likewise in Matt. 28:20, the two-step process for making disciples for Jesus, is baptizing them and *"teaching them to observe all that I commanded you."* He did not say, "Teach them all that I commanded you!"—that would take years!

All we are looking for prior to baptism is consent: *"I agree to obey Jesus in everything—whatever that involves!"* This goes a long way toward defining what Jesus was after when He declared: *"If anyone wishes to come after Me, he must deny himself, and take up his cross daily and follow Me. For whoever wishes to save his life will lose it, but whoever loses his life for My sake, he is the one who will save it"* (Luke 9:23-24, NASB). The sacrifice is so demanding and consuming that it qualifies as a "death"—the absolute fatality of the autonomous self! This is confirmed by 2 Cor. 5:14-15—*"For the love of Christ controls us, having concluded this, that one died for all, therefore all died; and He died for all, so that they who live might no longer live for themselves, but for Him who died and rose again on their behalf."*

The death I have just described is real; it is no fiction. Accepting this death is necessary before baptism as a prerequisite—otherwise we would have the baptism of one who has never bowed to the Lordship of Jesus!

Paper money has value because it is backed by something like gold—otherwise the dollar is just paper. Baptism is backed by the death of the convert—otherwise it is just "getting-wet-all-over"! The death is formalized (by God) at the moment one is buried under baptismal waters, and this death is not optional! The Christian who will emerge from that grave will no longer be self-willed, but will live to obey the will of Jesus. He or she will then have "obeyed the gospel"!

Death to Sin

The baptismal death is a death to self; it is also a death to sin! Baptism not only washes away previously committed sins; it prevents new sins from being committed. This is the finely woven message of Romans 6 and 8. Sins are now avoided and prevented. The slavery under sin has ended in liberation. This happens for two reasons. First, where there has been a death to self, Jesus is now in control—of course sin cannot be practiced any longer:

> *Everyone who practices sin also practices lawlessness; and sin is lawlessness. You know that He appeared in order to take away sins; and in Him there is no sin. No one who abides in Him sins; no one who sins has seen Him or knows Him. Little children, make sure no one deceives you; the one who practices righteousness is righteous, just as He is righteous; the one who practices sin is of the devil; for the devil has sinned from the beginning. The Son of God appeared for this purpose, to destroy the works of the devil. No one who is born of God practices sin, because His seed abides in him; and he cannot sin, because he is born of God. By this the children of God and the children of the devil are obvious: anyone who does not practice righteousness is not of God, nor the one who does not love his brother.* (1 John 3:4-10, NASB)

Second, sin stops because weakness is replaced with strength! The old self lived "by the flesh," a condition of spiritual weakness.

That person was simply not strong enough to withstand the power of sin. But that weak person dies in baptism...and in his or her place a "new self" emerges as though by baptismal resurrection! Before emerging in "new birth," God places His Holy Spirit within the heart as a source of power, sanctification, and transformation into the image of Jesus. Sin and temptation have been torn down as the dominant power!

So, in baptism there is the death of the believer—a death to sin and to self. But that death morphs into or fuses with the death of Jesus. Each of them—Jesus and the convert—has been crucified. But they are so joined by the experience of mutual self-sacrifice that it is as though they are crucified on the same cross:

> *Or do you not know that all of us who have been baptized into Christ Jesus have been <u>baptized into His death</u>? Therefore we have been <u>buried with Him</u> through baptism into death, so that as Christ was raised from the dead through the glory of the Father, so we too might walk in newness of life. For if we have become <u>united with Him in the likeness of His death</u>, cer-*

> tainly we shall also be in the likeness of His resurrection, knowing this, that our old self was <u>crucified with Him</u>, in order that our body of sin might be done away with, so that we would no longer be slaves to sin; for he who has died is freed from sin. Now <u>if we have died with Christ</u>, we believe that we shall also live with Him, knowing that Christ, having been raised from the dead, is never to die again; death no longer is master over Him. For the death that He died, He died to sin once for all; but the life that He lives, He lives to God. Even so <u>consider yourselves to be dead to sin</u>, but alive to God in Christ Jesus. (Romans 6:3-11, NASB).

I have said all this to warn against a competing theology of baptism. It finds the single death of Jesus on the Cross to be the only actual death—and believers are baptized into it. The "second cross" to which we are nailed (death to self and to sin) is never given attention. In this view, baptism into His death allows the believer contact with the sin-washing blood and so sins are forgiven. Nothing is required of the convert except immersion in water. You may have to read that twice because the two theologies sound alike. But I am not splitting hairs. The Bible declares a covenant-relationship that elicits supreme sacrifice from BOTH partners—both Jesus and His converts must bear a cross! In the other view, Jesus alone is crucified and the convert gets the reward without a matching death of his own!

Let agreement be fully given to all that this alternative theology affirms; but solid disagreement to what it denies. Agreed: that baptism is the place where we join Jesus in His death-experience and find salvation in His crucifixion! In baptism, sins are washed away by the blood of Jesus. Denied: that one may be baptized without experiencing total self-sacrifice for himself, and the "death" which this entails! In our work of evangelism, to fail to require the convert to suffer his own "death" so shortens the "magnitude of the step" that it strips away the conversionary requirements laid down by Jesus. A convert—who does not die—fails to "obey the gospel"!

Let me address a possible criticism. Someone might complain that the "two cross" theology, advocated here, makes it sound as though "two saviors" are required for salvation. And, to some ears, it may sound as though the crucified Jesus made no greater contribution than does the convert.

That is *not* what we are saying.

If two-cross theology "sounds like" this, it is because our view is truly relational, truly covenantal—that takes two partners. But there is crucial distinction between His Cross and our cross. Only Jesus' crucifixion accomplishes atonement, as the reparative act that reverses the damage of sin, making forgiveness possible. We do not deserve His death for us (see the grace here); but Jesus deserves the ultimate sacrifice from us (see our response to grace here)! His sacrifice is perfect, unblemished, and complete; even when we give our utmost and absolute best in response, our sacrifice is flawed and terribly incomplete. All of these distinctions are bound up in the New Covenant—and so is the necessity for two crosses.

A Right Reading of Romans

To get theology wrong in a one-cross way, one must misread Romans 6. This "single-death theology" misses the thrust of this chapter of Scripture. The "newness of life" in v. 4 is often understood incorrectly and it is key to interpretation. "Newness of life" is taken to mean something like salvation, the equivalent of eternal life. Get baptized and—because Jesus died—death loses finality and you are given "newness of life" that is eternal. All of that is true. But this is not Paul's meaning in this chapter!

Paul wants his readers to understand "newness of life" in a way that tends to the question that opens the chapter: *"What shall we say then? <u>Are we to continue in sin</u> so that grace may increase?"* The answer clearly expected is not merely negative, but emphatically negative: *"God forbid! Anathema!"* And the reason? Because baptism that contacts Christ's death also involves your own death—death to self, death to sin! This results (or, at least, should have resulted) in "newness of life"! And it should be clear that Paul uses this expression to indicate a newly "sanctified" quality of life—life that is ethically purified; life in which sin no longer has a place. It refuses to *"continue in sin."* This must be the correct understanding because it leads to this later in the chapter: *"Therefore do not let sin reign in your mortal body so that you obey its lusts, and do not go on presenting the members of your body to sin as instruments of unrighteousness; but present* *yourselves to God as those alive from the dead, and your members as instruments of righteousness to God. For sin shall not be master over you, for you are not under law but under grace"* (6:12-14). To grasp Paul's meaning, the "two deaths" must be kept in view.

Let's try another approach. There are two ways for a sinner to become holy (or sanctified). One is to find God's forgiveness for *sins already committed.* The other way to find holiness is to avoid committing them at all and in the first place—those sins would have surely been committed had we never died with Christ! Before baptism we lived in the weakness of "the flesh" and we were powerless to resist sin. In Romans 6, the apostle's focus is on the second way to holiness— refusing to commit sins!

Notice that the other viewpoint, which we oppose, entirely relies on "forgiven" sins (and we also affirm that, even after baptism—1 John 1:7ff.). However, it weakens on the "refusing" of future sins and never admits power for the Christian to win over sin. Refusing sin is something a baptized believer "ought" to do, they would affirm without hesitation (and we agree). Yet Paul would insist that a

Christian, having died to sin with Christ, "must" win the sin-battle. There is a huge difference here between "ought" and "must"—it is the difference between a convert who has taken up his own cross, and another who has not!

To follow Paul's thought forward in Romans, Chapter Seven will discuss his failure to win the sin-battle and identifies that failure with "living according to the flesh" (v. 5). Paul discusses this as his own firsthand experience (vs. 7ff.)—he himself once lived *"according to the flesh."* That experience for Paul was an experience of failure! His every intention to obey God through the Law ended, instead, with sin! Paul's description is one of slavery! Some may think this experience of failure (in Chapter Seven) should be understood as an expected feature of Christian life. When a Christian gets overpowered by sin, it should be considered a "normal" part of Christian spirituality? We believe that this interpretation emerges only through a misreading of Romans.

We do better if we understand that Paul, in Chapter Seven, is not narrating his experience *as a Christian* (who now is free from the Jewish Law). Rather, he describes the experience he had before becoming a Christian! That failure—always losing to sin—was experienced BEFORE Paul was baptized into Christ! He describes the experience he had while living under the Law BEFORE entering New Covenant with Jesus. Chapter Seven cannot be read as "normal" Christian spiritual experience without creating direct contradiction with what Paul writes in the chapter before (Six) and after (Eight). Contradiction? Yes, between the victorious breaking of sin's enslaving power in Six and Eight, against the defeat under sin in total weakness in Seven. That contradiction is irreconcilable!

In Chapter Six, being overpowered by sin is brought to an end in baptism. After Chapter Seven, discussion turns from fleshly failure to Christian success—and victory over the sin-battle—in Chapter Eight. Here, victory is now possible because the Holy Spirit indwells baptized Christians, infusing them with power not available to other (fleshly) mortals. This power gives ability to win over sin, and obligates Christians with greater responsibility to walk "in newness of life." In another Scripture with the same thought:

> *For this is the will of God, your sanctification;* that is, that you abstain from sexual immorality; that each of you know how to possess his own vessel in sanctification and honor, not in lustful passion, like the Gentiles who do not know God; and that no man transgress and defraud his brother in the matter because the Lord is the avenger in all these things, just as we also told you before and solemnly warned you. For God has not called us for the purpose of impurity, but in sanctification. So, *he who rejects this is not rejecting man but the God who gives His Holy Spirit to you.* (1 Thessalonians 4:3-8)

Notice in this passage that Paul's expectation for "sanctification" is tied to the successful refusal of future sins, to preventing sin from happening in the first place. And, the power to accomplish this—in Romans 8—comes from the Holy Spirit.

Obeying The Gospel, Redux

Without a death-experience of your own (that is triggered by a powerful response to the Cross-death-experience of Jesus), a thousand immersions in water will not save. His death was a from-the-heart "sacrifice" for you! Without matching His sacrifice with your own limitless sacrifice offered to Him, baptism is robbed of significance. This is what it means to "obey the gospel." It is not enough to get "get-wet-all-over" into the death of Jesus without dying yourself. Evangelism that does not answer the Cross of Lord Jesus with a cross for the convert fails. The "magnitude of the step" required here is simply too small to result in conversion. Jesus himself declares that anyone who wants to follow without his or her own cross-death *"cannot be my disciple"* (Luke 14:27). Paul's trustworthy statement is absolutely conditional: *"For if we died with Him, we will also live with Him"* (2 Timothy 2:11).

Two Ways of Evangelism

The "one cross" and "two cross" theologies share many points of contact and therefore look very similar. How can you tell which theology underlies various methodologies of evangelism?

Listen to what is emphasized! Evangelism based on "one cross" will emphasize *what the believer gets* from conversion; evangelism based on "two cross" theology will go on also to emphasize *what a believer must give!* Both promise salvation, forgiveness from sins, eternal life. Both anchor this in atonement through Jesus' crucifixion (His Cross). But only one requires the believing convert to die as well, as prerequisite to baptism. The other also requires baptism, but emphasizes contact with His death—while going silent on dying to self and to sin.

The "one cross" approach seems to have the advantage: its offer is huge in benefits while its demands are small—five (or six) easy steps and eternal life is yours! Will this approach be more attractive to unbelievers, and therefore more successful? No—for two reasons. First, as we argued earlier in this book, imposing a huge relational demand is more congruous with the huge gains and advantages that attach to Christian conversion—and this gives "two cross" evangelism a rightful air of authenticity. The higher demand will attract more takers. Second, the easy sell of the "one cross" methodology, even should it result in more baptisms, would be judged a failure by the one whose judgment matters: Jesus! Only the "two cross" theology brings converts to "obey the gospel" and weds them to God in the New Covenant.

A FINAL WORD

The aim of this book is to enable successful evangelism by building upon truly Biblical theology with a methodology that is simple and effective. Our final word together will offer reasons why you should "get after it" and work this method yourself.

First, because we reach back into the Bible for God's evangelistic strategy. It seems we in modernity have set aside the "radical demands" of Jesus for would-be disciples and converts. We set them aside because we did not know what to do with them! Perhaps we even wanted to soften them to enhance the gospel's appeal. These demands stand opposite the lite-and-trite *"just accept the Lord Jesus into your heart"* that is the essence of evangelistic conversion among many denominations. Forget "accepting Jesus"—our approach aims at establishing the relationship by which Jesus accepts us! Those neglected Scriptures are reclaimed here into the very heart of both the theology and methodology of Three Square Evangelism. Our approach to soul-winning again sets high the bar!

Second, because by now you should have confidence that you are capable of working the method *with a little practice.* "You can do this!" That encouragement was dropped for you at each of the Three Squares, and you must know you are capable! After reducing the whole procedure to a simple outline, we spelled out the few preparations you need to make to ready yourself.

Some readers will fail to get to Square One. Determine that you won't be among them!

Re-visit that list of preparations. Practice. Rehearse. Role-play. Work out the entire Three Square process in your mind. Work out the easy transitions from one completed Square to the next. Do that in private until you are comfortable and ready to raise the question: *"Can you tell me what a Christian is?"* Once you grasp the flow you will become sure-footed, knowing all through the process where to go next, and how to get there.

Third, because at each Square you will find what you need for success—focus, power, salvation! Jesus has your back! He's got this! **Focus** keeps the process from wandering who-knows-where. You will feel like you are in control. **Power** comes from God, from the Cross. That takes pressure off of you. **Salva-**

tion is easy after the convert has responded to the Cross!

Fourth, because the challenge level for Christians is rising. It is no longer a badge of honor in our culture to identify as a Christian. Persecution and opposition to faith are on the rise. Three Square Evangelism creates strong Christians. They have already died for Jesus. They have counted the cost that demands full self-sacrifice, and are agreed. They know Jesus as Lord. The days are past when those sprung from "soft conversions" could get by without a soul-threatening challenge. Our day calls for Christians built of solid faith, established convictions, and unwavering commitment.

Read 1 Corinthians 3:10-15. Paul warns that everyone doing evangelistic work will see their efforts "tested by fire." Evangelism done poorly will be burned up, destroyed! Some work is built of flammable materials and it will not hold up against destructive forces. Sometimes, even quality workmanship ends in ashes. However, some of us will build with flame-proof materials when we evangelize. Our converts will show forth faith that cannot be destroyed by temptation, ridicule, suffering, peer pressure, or the fires of persecution. They tend to be fireproof!

Three Square Evangelism is built tough! Jesus issued radical demands that guarantee that any that follow Him are battle ready! We offer salvation only to those who face Jesus on the Cross, count the high cost of a response, and ask for a cross of their own on which to be nailed! These are the kind of people on which a solid church fellowship may be built. They make good soldiers, and good servants.

No evangelism, no conversion can be guaranteed against failure. The Parable of the Sower says that every scattered seed lands atop soils of varying quality. We all face the potential of failure. However, we can have some control over the quality of our workmanship in evangelism. When we get a conversion, no one should claim ignorance about the requirements for dying to sin and to self. None should say, "I had no idea Christian living would demand so much of me!" In some popular methods, converts are not prepared for these challenges. The focus was on a "getting saved" that emphasized only what Jesus suffered and sacrificed. They wilt when things get tough, and all that remains of the conversion is a pile of ashes.

Three Square Evangelism offers the greatest chance for success. You should not give up until you are able to make it work yourself. Get to Square One and see it through.

You can do this!

www.ingramcontent.com/pod-product-compliance
Lightning Source LLC
Chambersburg PA
CBHW071259040426
42444CB00009B/1784